# ICE CREAM

*gelatos* ◆ *ices* ◆ *sherbets* ◆ *sorbets*

# FOR ALL SEASONS

Deb Tomasi and Suzy Gardner

## *ReTreat Publishing*

**Appleton, WI ◆ Boulder, CO**

**Printing History**
*First Edition      May 1999*

All inquiries should be addressed to:
**ReTreat Publishing**
**2115 Harvest Drive**
**Appleton, WI  54914**

ISBN:  0-9670448-0-4
Library of Congress:  99-93112

*Cover Photographs:*
*Lemon Sherbet (pg. 15), Watermelon Sorbet (pg. 41), Pumpkin Spice Ice Cream (pg. 52), Fruitcake Ice Cream (pg. 80)*

# ACKNOWLEDGEMENTS

*Without our supportive families this dream would not be a reality. They have inspired our love for cooking, our individuality, and our sense of purpose in life.*

*We would also like to recognize the many individuals for their roles in making our book possible.*

*Rico, Brittany, and Micaela Tomasi*
*Dan, Emily, and Erin Gardner*
*Charles, Barbara, Rich, Suzanne, and Ed Wise*
*Marilyn Taylor*
*Holly Wallace*
*Teddy Thorel*
*Vince and Doreen Tomasi*
*Janice Brown*
*Ron, Aline, Rodney, and Mary Weber*
*The Lietzke Family*
*The Ziehr Family*
*Allie Matthies*
*Roger Burris*
*Jeff Kamps*

# TABLE OF CONTENTS

## *Introduction*

**1**

Introduction ◆ Ice Cream Basics ◆ Types of Frozen Treats ◆ Types of Ice Cream Makers ◆ Kitchen Tools ◆ Ingredients ◆ Processing ◆ Packing and Storing ◆ Serving

## *Spring Recipes*

**7**

Classic Vanilla Ice Cream ◆ Classic Chocolate Ice Cream ◆ Classic Strawberry Ice Cream ◆ Spumoni Ice Cream ◆ Strawberry Cheesecake Ice Cream ◆ Pistachio Ice Cream ◆ Lime Sherbet ◆ Coconut Ice Cream ◆ Lemon Sherbet ◆ Strawberry Daiquiri Ice ◆ Painkiller Ice ◆ Peachy Wine Ice ◆ Blueberry Ice ◆ Raspberry Mascarpone Ice Cream ◆ Maple Walnut Ice Cream ◆ Nanaimo Ice Cream ◆ Pineapple Sherbet ◆ Chocolate Cherry Sherbet ◆ Ginger Peach Ice Cream ◆ Coconut Candy Bar Ice Cream

## *Summer Recipes*

**29**

Banana Dream Ice Cream ◆ Peanut Butter Ice Cream ◆ Rocky Road Ice Cream ◆ Key Lime Ice Cream ◆ Orange Sherbet ◆ Cantaloupe Ice Cream ◆ Honey Vanilla Ice Cream ◆ Citrus Ice ◆ Kiwi Delight Sherbet ◆ Blackberry Sorbet ◆ Apricot White Chocolate Ice Cream ◆ Ginger Plum Ice Cream ◆ Watermelon Sorbet ◆ Peach Sherbet ◆ Island Delight Ice Cream ◆ Cream Soda Sherbet ◆ Papaya Gelato ◆ Sunset Gelato ◆ Blueberry Ice Cream ◆ Suzy's "Your Choice" Ice Cream

# TABLE OF CONTENTS

## Fall Recipes
### 51

Spiced Apple Ice Cream ◆ Pumpkin Spice Ice Cream ◆ Cranberry Ice ◆ Cider Ice ◆ Orange Spiced Tea Ice Cream ◆ Pecan Praline Ice Cream ◆ Chocolate Chip Cookie Dough Ice Cream ◆ Spice Ice Cream ◆ Gingered Pear Sorbet ◆ Orange Cream with Spiced Pecans Ice Cream ◆ Persimmon Ice Cream ◆ Cinnamon Stick Ice Cream ◆ Butter Pecan Ice Cream ◆ Toasted Almond Ice Cream ◆ Butterscotch Ice Cream ◆ Cappucino Gelato ◆ Cranberry Raspberry Sorbet ◆ Pumpkin Cheesecake Ice Cream ◆ Fig Ice Cream ◆ Cannoli Ice Cream

## Winter Recipes
### 73

Kiss Me Again Chocolate Ice Cream ◆ Mint Chocolate Chip Ice Cream ◆ Mimosa Ice ◆ Red Wine Ice Cream ◆ Peppermint Ice Cream ◆ White Chocolate Cherry Ice Cream ◆ Egg Nog Ice Cream ◆ Fruitcake Ice Cream ◆ Tiramisu Ice Cream ◆ White Chocolate Macadamia Nut Ice Cream ◆ Rum Raisin Ice Cream ◆ Grasshopper Ice Cream ◆ Mocha Ice Cream ◆ Vanilla Bean Ice Cream ◆ Amaretto Ice Cream ◆ Red Currant Ice Cream ◆ Triple Chocolate Overload Ice Cream ◆ Green Tea Ice Cream ◆ Deb's Your Choice Ice Cream ◆ Dark Chocolate Cheesecake Ice Cream

## Index
### 93

# Introduction

For us, the kitchen is a place to escape to; it is a place for creativity, adventure, and renewal. We strive for quick and enjoyable ways to work with the freshest seasonal ingredients we can find. Combining that spirit with a love for sweets (and a new ice cream maker!), our adventure began. We were inspired to create a cookbook featuring unique, yet easy to make, frozen goodies prepared in an electric ice cream maker. For this writing, we chose a theme that carries through all seasons enabling you to take advantage of fresh seasonal ingredients. Now you can enjoy ice cream all year long!

The process of making ice cream is quite simple; it requires only a few basic ingredients and takes very little time. The recipes in this book are made with a 1 1/2 quart electric ice cream maker using items that are widely available. There is no special talent required to produce ice cream, and the results are desserts to be proud of. We hope you are inspired to enjoy the traditional recipes as well as seek to create what has yet to be created.

## Ice Cream Basics

The recipe development phase of this endeavor proved to be an enormous amount of fun. We would discuss flavors, depart to our individual kitchens, then regroup for the indescribable tasting sessions. Not only are the recipes delicious, they are works of art in their own sense.

You may be asking yourself, "why make my own?" For approximately the same price as premium store brands, you can make a better tasting and fresher product with no preservatives. You can enjoy seasonal favorites using the freshest ingredients available. When it comes to making your own ice cream, the possibilities are endless; making your own enables you to be creative. There is also the benefit of stocking your freezer with the flavors you, your family, and your friends enjoy most. Imagine the fun you can have with recipe creation!

## Types of Frozen Treats

Our book focuses on ice cream recipes; but, for a little added interest we've also included recipes for some gelatos, sherbets, sorbets, and ices. *Ice Cream* is typically made with whole eggs, or egg yolks, and heavy cream. The use of eggs and heavy cream produces the richest creamiest product. *Gelato* is an Italian ice cream made with milk. Gelatos are not as creamy as traditional ice creams, since milk has a lower fat content than heavy cream. Both *Sherbet and Sorbet* are made without egg yolks; in some of our recipes, they do contain egg whites. Sherbets and sorbets are made with milk, half and half, or heavy cream. The result is a more icy, yet still somewhat creamy, product. Finally, *Ices* consist primarily of fruit and fruit juices and contain no eggs, heavy cream, half and half, or milk.

## Types of Ice Cream Makers

There are many manufacturers of electric ice cream makers. Most department and kitchen specialty stores carry at least one model. They can also be purchased through kitchen specialty catalogs and in many stores on the internet. At this writing, prices started around $40 and most models were priced under $80. To make the recipes in this book, we recommend a 1 1/2 quart **electric** ice cream maker (**not** the type of machine that requires ice and salt). We highly recommend familiarizing yourself with your machine's instruction materials before attempting to make ice cream.

## Kitchen Tools

In addition to your electric ice cream maker, some basic kitchen tools and supplies are helpful to have on hand when making ice cream. Most recipes require a blender, food processor, standing mixer, or mixing bowl and whisk. Also required are standard measuring cups, spoons, spatulas, and a saucepan or two. It is helpful to have a good sharp knife for chopping nuts and some sort of grater for grating chocolate; a food processor with the appropriate attachments is ideal. Finally, freezer proof containers and plastic wrap are needed for storing your ice cream in the freezer.

## Ingredients

The freshest ingredients and quality products are essential to producing good ice cream. The ingredients listed below are commonly used in our recipes and are good items to have on hand for that spur of the moment batch of ice cream.

Eggs (large, grade A or AA) ◆ Heavy Cream (whipping cream is a good substitute) ◆ Half and Half ◆ Milk ◆ Fresh Fruit ◆ Sugar (white, unless otherwise specified) ◆ Canned Fruit or Pie Filling ◆ Chocolate Bars (premium brand) ◆ Cocoa Powder ◆ Spices ◆ Nuts ◆ Extracts (vanilla, peppermint) ◆ Liqueurs

In our test kitchens, we tried substituting fat free half and half and lactose reduced milk products for their higher fat equivalents. While the end result was a less creamy, more icy, product the taste was still quite good.

## Processing

Process the ice cream according to the manufacturer's instructions. To ensure the best results, be sure that your tub is properly frozen and that your ingredients, where possible, are well chilled. You should also note that most ice cream is not frozen solid immediately after processing; the consistency is usually more like a soft serve product. Simply freeze the ice cream for 4-6 hours to achieve a solid texture.

It is also important to note that the use of alcohol inhibits the freezing process. A few of our recipes call for the addition of a small amount of liquor. Be sure to measure the alcohol precisely and add it at the end of the processing cycle unless otherwise indicated.

## Packing and Storing

Since most of the recipes yield a little more than 1 quart, have 1 1/2 quart freezer containers on hand for storage. Pour the processed ice cream into a container, cover with plastic wrap, secure the lid, and label with the flavor and date. Store the ice cream in the deepest part of your freezer, if possible, where it is coldest. Homemade ice cream tastes best when eaten within 7-10 days. If you are packing the ice cream to take to a party or for gift giving, try using the new "disposable" storage containers. For an extra festive touch, wrap the container in colored plastic wrap and tie with a ribbon.

## Serving

Prior to serving, remove ice cream from the freezer and let stand at room temperature for 10-15 minutes. This allows the ice cream to soften slightly and the flavors to come to life. Be creative with presentation. Use colorful plates or bowls and garnish with nuts or edible flowers. Serve on a plain white plate dusted with cocoa powder or drizzled with chocolate or raspberry sauce. Don't overlook the elegance of serving in a champagne flute, wine glass, or brandy snifter. An ice cream that looks great tastes even better!

# Spring

# Classic Vanilla
## Ice Cream

*This classic vanilla ice cream makes a wonderful foundation for any sundae creation, or to simply savor alone.*

| | |
|---|---|
| **4 egg yolks** | **2 cups heavy cream** |
| **1 cup sugar** | **2 cups half and half** |
| **2 tsp. vanilla extract** | |

In a large bowl, beat the egg yolks.  While continuing to beat, gradually add the sugar, vanilla, heavy cream, and half and half.

Process in ice cream maker according to manufacturer's instructions.

**Yield:  Slightly more than 1 quart**

# Classic Chocolate
### Ice Cream

*This is a quick and delicious version of chocolate ice cream.*

| | |
|---|---|
| **4 egg yolks** | **2 tsp. vanilla extract** |
| **1 cup sugar** | **1 cup heavy cream** |
| **1/3 cup cocoa powder** | **2 cups half and half** |

In a large bowl, beat the egg yolks.  While continuing to beat, gradually add the sugar.  Add the cocoa powder and vanilla; blend well.  Finally, beat in the heavy cream and half and half.

Process in ice cream maker according to manufacturer's instructions.

**Yield:  1 quart**

*Variations:  For <u>Chocolate Walnut Ice Cream</u>, add 1 cup of chopped walnuts in final minutes of processing. For <u>Double Chocolate Walnut Ice Cream</u>, add 1 cup of chopped walnuts AND 1/2 cup of chocolate shavings in final minutes of processing.*

# Classic Strawberry
## Ice Cream

*Nothing says spring like a big bowl of fresh strawberry ice cream! We think the homemade version of this classic recipe far surpasses any store bought brand.*

| | |
|---|---|
| 1 pint strawberries (2 cups) | 3 eggs |
| 2 Tbsp. orange juice | 2 cups heavy cream |
| 1 1/4 cups sugar, divided | 1/2 cup half and half |

In a large bowl, combine the strawberries, orange juice, and 1/2 cup of the sugar. Let sit at room temperature for 15 minutes. In a blender or food processor, puree the strawberry mixture to a consistency you desire in the ice cream. (We like some chunks.)

In another large bowl, beat the eggs until light and fluffy. Add the heavy cream, half and half, and strawberry puree. Mix well.

Process in ice cream maker according to manufacturer's instructions.

**Yield:  Slightly more than 1 quart**

*Variations:  For __Strawberry Chocolate Chip Ice Cream__, add 3/4 cup of chocolate chips in final minutes of processing. For __Strawberry Pie Ice Cream__, add 3/4 cup of graham cracker pieces in final minutes of processing.*

# Spumoni
## Ice Cream

*Spumoni is a flavor I grew up knowing well, since it is a favorite of my parents. In fact, their favorite dessert at their favorite restaraunt in Canada is Spumoni. After tasting this recipe, I'm sure you'll share their enthusiasm for the flavor.   Deb*

1-3.4 oz. package pistachio instant pudding mix
3 eggs
1/2 cup sugar
1 cup heavy cream
2 1/2 cups half and half
1/3 cup chopped nuts

1/4 cup strawberries, chopped
1/4 cup maraschino cherries, chopped
1/8 cup candied fruit
3 Tbsp. rum
1/2 cup chocolate syrup

In a blender or food processor, combine the first 5 ingredients (pudding through half and half). Mix well.

Process in ice cream maker according to manufacturer's instructions. Add the nuts, strawberries, cherries, candied fruit, and rum in final minutes of processing.

To pack: Spread 1/3 of the ice cream in a 2 1/2 quart freezer container. Top with 1/4 cup of the chocolate syrup. Repeat to form a second layer and top with the remaining ice cream.

**Yield: Slightly more than 2 quarts**

# Strawberry Cheesecake
## Ice Cream

*Cheesecake flavored ice cream combines two desserts that everyone loves - cheesecake and ice cream.  This recipe calls for strawberries, but the possibilities for additions to the basic cheesecake ice cream are endless.  Experiment!*

| | |
|---|---|
| **3/4 cup chopped strawberries** | **2 cups heavy cream** |
| **1 1/4 cups sugar, divided** | **1 cup half and half** |
| **2 Tbsp. orange juice** | **8 oz. cream cheese, softened** |
| **3 eggs** | |

In a small bowl, combine the strawberries, 1/2 cup of sugar, and orange juice.  Set aside.  In a blender or food processor, combine the remaining ingredients EXCEPT strawberry mixture.  Mix well.

Process in ice cream maker according to manufacturer's instructions.

Strain the strawberries and discard the juice.  Add the berries in final minutes of processing.

**Yield:  Slightly more than 1 quart**

# Pistachio
## Ice Cream

*Since my husband often has pistachios around the house to munch on, this recipe evolved quite naturally.  It's a richly textured dessert that has a wonderful pistachio flavor and crunch.    Suzy*

3 eggs
3/4 cup sugar
2 cups heavy cream
1 cup half and half

1 tsp. vanilla extract
4-5 drops green food coloring (optional)
1 cup shelled pistachios

In a blender or food processor, combine all of the ingredients EXCEPT pistachios.  Mix well.  Add the pistachios and process for another 15 seconds.  You want to incorporate the pistachio flavor without completely pulverizing the nuts.

Process in ice cream maker according to manufacturer's instructions.

**Yield:  Slightly more than 1 quart**

# Lime
## Sherbet

*This flavor is best enjoyed when fresh lime juice is used. Fortunately, limes are available year round so this sherbet can be enjoyed anytime.*

**4 egg whites**
**1 1/4 cups sugar**
**1 cup heavy cream**

**2 cups half and half**
**1/2 cup fresh lime juice (4-5 limes)**
**4-5 drops green food coloring (optional)**

In a large bowl, beat the egg whites until frothy. While continuing to beat, gradually add the sugar and beat until glossy. Stir in the heavy cream, half and half, and lime juice. Add food coloring, if desired. Mix well.

Process in ice cream maker according to manufacturer's instructions.

**Yield: Slightly more than 1 quart**

# Coconut
## Ice Cream

*This is a rich and creamy ice cream bursting with coconut flavor.  Enjoy it alone or make a great pina colada by combining some of the ice cream with a little rum and chopped pineapple in a blender!*

| | |
|---|---|
| **3 eggs** | **1 1/2 cups half and half** |
| **3/4 cup sugar** | **1-16 oz. can cream of coconut** |
| **1 cup heavy cream** | |

In a blender or food processor, combine all of the ingredients.  Mix well.

Process in ice cream maker according to manufacturer's instructions.  (Note:  Ice cream may only freeze to a slushy state due to the oil in the cream of coconut.  Simply pour the slush into a container and freeze.)

**Yield:  Slightly more than 1 quart**

*Variations:  For **Double Coconut Ice Cream**, add 3/4 cup of toasted coconut in final minutes of processing. (To toast coconut:  Spread in a thin layer on a cookie sheet and bake in a 350 degree oven.  Watch carefully, stirring every couple of minutes.  Remove when the coconut is lightly browned.)*

# Lemon
## Sherbet

*This sherbet is a classic.  Serve with an assortment of cookies for a simple springtime dessert.*

| | |
|---|---|
| **4 egg whites** | **1 1/2 cups half and half** |
| **1 cup sugar** | **3/4 cup fresh lemon juice (4-5 lemons)** |
| **1 cup heavy cream** | **3-4 drops yellow food coloring (optional)** |

In a large bowl, beat the egg whites until frothy.  While continuing to beat, gradually add the sugar and beat until glossy.  Stir in the heavy cream, half and half, and lemon juice.  Add food coloring, if desired.  Mix well.

Process in ice cream maker according to manufacturer's instructions.

**Yield:  Slightly more than 1 quart**

# Strawberry Daiquiri
## Ice

*This recipe was developed in honor of some friends who love their "fruity slushy drinks!" Eating a dish of this is like eating a frozen daiquiri.     Suzy*

> **1 1/2 pints (3 cups) fresh or frozen (defrosted) strawberries**
> **2 Tbsp. orange juice**
> **2/3 cup sugar**
> **2 cups cold water**
> **1/4 cup light corn syrup**
> **1/4 cup rum**

In a large bowl, combine the strawberries, orange juice, and sugar. Let sit at room temperature for 10-15 minutes. In a blender or food processor, puree the mixture to desired consistency. Return the strawberry puree to the bowl; add the water and corn syrup. Whisk to mix well.

Process in ice cream maker according to manufacturer's instructions.

Add the rum in final minute of processing.

**Yield: 1 quart**

# Painkiller
## Ice

*The painkiller is a popular libation in the British Virgin Islands. My first experience with a painkiller was on the island of Virgin Gorda; the drink, however, is rumored to have originated on the island of Jost Van Dyke. Deb*

1 1/2 cups cold water
1 cup pineapple juice
1 cup orange juice

2/3 cup cream of coconut
1/8 cup dark rum

In a large bowl, combine the cold water, juices, and cream of coconut. Whisk to mix well.

Process in ice cream maker according to manufacturer's instructions.

Add the rum in final minute of processing.

**Yield: Slightly more than 1 quart**

# Peachy Wine
## Ice

*This is an easy and tasty way to use up leftover white wine.  Use a good quality wine for the best results.  A light and slightly sweet Riesling is perfect.*

**2 cups fresh peaches (peeled, pitted, and sliced), OR
2 cups canned peaches, drained
3/4 cup powdered sugar
2 Tbsp. orange juice
1 cup cold water
3/4 cup white wine
1/3 cup light corn syrup**

In a blender or food processor, combine all of the ingedients.  Mix well.

Process in ice cream maker according to manufacturer's instructions.  (Note:  Mixture may only freeze to a slushy state, due to the alcohol.  Simply pour the slush into a container and freeze.)

**Yield:  Slightly more than 1 quart**

*Variations:  For* **Plum Wine Ice***, substitute canned plums that have been seeded and diced for the peaches.*

# Blueberry
## Ice

*This recipe is as beautiful as it is delicious.  The rich blue-purple color needs only the simplest of garnishes.  Serve in a white or crystal bowl with a sprig of mint.*

**2 cups fresh or frozen (defrosted) blueberries**
**1/2 cup sugar**
**3 Tbsp. orange juice**
**2 cups cold water**
**1/3 cup light corn syrup**

In a small saucepan, combine the blueberries, sugar, and orange juice. Cook over medium heat, uncovered, for 10 minutes.  Stir occasionally.  Let cool.  In a blender or food processor, combine the cooled blueberry mixture, water, and corn syrup.  Mix well.

Process in ice cream maker according to manufacturer's instructions.

**Yield:  1 quart**

# Raspberry Mascarpone
## Ice Cream

*The mascarpone cheese in this recipe produces an unbelievably rich and creamy ice cream.*

| | |
|---|---|
| **1 cup whole raspberries** | **1 tsp. vanilla extract** |
| **1 1/2 cups sugar, divided** | **8 oz. mascarpone cheese** |
| **3 egg yolks** | **1 cup heavy cream** |
| **1/8 tsp. salt** | **1 cup half and half** |

In a small bowl, gently stir 1/2 cup of the sugar into the raspberries; set aside. In a large mixing bowl, beat the egg yolks. While continuing to beat, gradually add the remaining sugar, salt, and vanilla. Add the mascarpone cheese and blend until creamy. Stir in the heavy cream and half and half. Mix well.

Process in ice cream maker according to manufacturer's instructions.

Add the raspberries, along with some of the juice, in final minutes of processing.

**Yield:  1 1/2 quarts**

*Variations:  For <u>Raspberry Truffle Ice Cream</u>, add 3/4 cup of grated chocolate in final minutes of processing. For <u>Raspberry Cheesecake Ice Cream</u>, substitute cream cheese for the mascarpone cheese.*

# Maple Walnut
## Ice Cream

*Maple walnut is a childhood favorite. Maple syrup and maple sugar candy are widely available in Canada; they are treats I grew up knowing and loving. This ice cream brings both sweets together. Rich maple flavored ice cream is accompanied by tiny nibbles of maple sugar candy.    Deb*

| | |
|---|---|
| **3 egg yolks** | **1 cup half and half** |
| **1/3 cup maple syrup** | **2/3 cup chopped walnuts** |
| **1/8 tsp. salt** | **1/3 cup crumbled maple sugar candy** |
| **2 cups heavy cream** | |

In a large bowl, beat the egg yolks. While continuing to beat, gradually add the maple syrup, salt, heavy cream, and half and half.

Process in ice cream maker according to manufacturer's instructions.

Add the walnuts and candy in final minutes of processing.

**Yield: 1 1/2 quarts**

*Variations: For **Maple Cream Ice Cream**, simply omit the walnuts. For **Maple Pecan Ice Cream**, substitute pecans for the walnuts. Toast the pecans, if you like.*

# Nanaimo
## Ice Cream

*This recipe is based on a traditional Canadian treat called the nanaimo bar.  If you are unable to find the custard powder (widely available in Canada), substitute 1-3.4 oz. package of vanilla pudding mix.    Deb*

1/2 cup butter, melted
1 cup sugar, divided
3 Tbsp. cocoa powder
1 tsp. vanilla extract
1 egg
1 cup graham cracker crumbs

1/2 cup coconut
1/4 cup chopped walnuts
3 egg yolks
3 Tbsp. custard powder (see above)
2 1/2 cups heavy cream
Chocolate hard shell topping

In a large saucepan, beat together the melted butter, 1/4 cup sugar, cocoa, vanilla, and 1 egg.  Cook over medium heat, stirring constantly, until the mixture reaches a custard consistency (2 to 3 minutes).  Remove from heat and add the cracker crumbs, coconut, and walnuts.  Press into an 8x8 pan and chill.  In a large bowl, beat the egg yolks with the remaining 3/4 cup sugar, custard powder, and heavy cream.

Process in ice cream maker according to manufacturer's instructions.

While the ice cream is processing, crumble the chilled chocolate mixture.  Add to ice cream in final minutes of processing.  Serve ice cream topped with the chocolate hard shell topping.

**Yield:  Slightly more than 1 1/2 quarts**

# Pineapple
## Sherbet

*Sherbets have always been a family favorite, especially when feeling a little under the weather. This recipe uses canned pineapple, so it can be enjoyed year round. For an exceptional treat, try using 2 cups of fresh pureed pineapple in place of the canned.    Deb*

**4 egg whites**                                     **2 Tbsp. lemon juice**
**1 cup sugar**                                      **1 cup half and half**
**1-20 oz. can crushed pineapple, undrained**

In a large mixing bowl, beat the egg whites until frothy. While continuing to beat, gradually add the sugar. Beat until stiff peaks form. Place the pineapple and lemon juice in a blender and puree. Transfer the pineapple to another large mixing bowl and stir in the half and half. Gently fold in the egg whites.

Process in ice cream maker according to manufacturer's instructions.

**Yield:  Slightly more than 1 quart**

# Chocolate Cherry
## Sherbet

*This sherbet is short on work but long on flavor! We were amazed by the rich and intense cherry flavor that the bottled cherry juice produced, and so easily.*

**3 cups unsweetened cherry juice**
**1 cup sugar**
**1 cup heavy cream**
**1 cup half and half**
**1 cup dark chocolate shavings or mini chocolate chips**

In a large saucepan, heat the cherry juice and sugar over medium heat. Stir until sugar dissolves. Let cool. In a blender or food processor, combine the cooled cherry juice, heavy cream, and half and half. Mix well.

Process in ice cream maker according to manufacturer's instructions.

Add the chocolate shavings or chips in final minutes of processing.

**Yield: Slightly more than 1 quart**

*Variations: For **Cherry Sherbet**, simply omit the chocolate shavings.*

# Ginger Peach
## Ice Cream

*While this may seem like a strange combination of ingredients, the result is a truly delicious and unique ice cream! It is an excellent dessert following a great Chinese dinner.*

**1 1/2 cups fresh peaches (peeled, pitted, and diced), OR
1-14.5 oz. can diced peaches, drained
3 eggs
3/4 cup sugar
2 cups heavy cream
1 cup half and half
3 1/2 tsp. ground ginger**

In a blender or food processor, combine all of the ingredients EXCEPT the peaches.  Mix well.

Process in ice cream maker according to manufacturer's instructions.

Add the peaches in final minutes of processing.

**Yield:  Slightly more than 1 quart**

# Coconut Candy Bar
## Ice Cream

*This recipe provides a great starting point for experimenting with adding your favorite candy bar pieces to ice cream.*

| | |
|---|---|
| 4 egg yolks | 1 cup heavy cream |
| 1 cup sugar | 1-14 oz. can coconut milk |
| 1 tsp. vanilla extract | 3/4 cup chopped coconut candy bars (about 2 standard size candy bars) |

In a large bowl, beat the egg yolks. While continuing to beat, gradually add the sugar, vanilla, heavy cream, and coconut milk.

Process in ice cream maker according to manufacturer's instructions.

Add the candy bar pieces in final minutes of processing.

**Yield: 1 1/2 quarts**

*Variations: For __Almond Coconut Candy Bar Ice Cream__, substitute 1/2 tsp. almond extract for the vanilla extract AND add 1/3 cup of chopped almonds in final minutes of processing. Toast the almonds for a little extra kick.*

# Summer

# Banana Dream
## Ice Cream

*This delicious ice cream is a big hit with both kids and adults. It's quite reminiscent of the banana pudding topped with vanilla wafers that most of our mothers made.*

| | |
|---|---|
| 1 cup mashed ripe banana | 2 eggs |
| Juice of 1/2 lemon | 1 tsp. vanilla extract |
| 1/3 cup sugar | 2 cups heavy cream |
| 1/8 tsp. salt | 1 cup half and half |

In a blender or food processor, combine all of the ingredients. Mix well.

Process in ice cream maker according to manufacturer's instructions.

**Yield: Slightly more than 1 quart**

*Variations: For __Banana Chocolate Chip Ice Cream__, add 3/4 cup of mini chocolate chips in final minutes of processing. For __Banana Nut Ice Cream__, add 3/4 cup of chopped walnuts OR toasted pecans in final minutes of processing.*

# Peanut Butter
### Ice Cream

*This recipe was one of the first developed.  We were bolstered by the success of having created a quick creamy treat that the whole family can enjoy.*

| | |
|---|---|
| **2/3 cup peanut butter*** | **2 cups heavy cream** |
| **3 eggs** | **1 cup half and half** |
| **3/4 cup sugar** | **1 Tbsp. vanilla extract** |

In a blender or food processor, combine all of the ingredients.  Mix well.

Process in ice cream maker according to manufacturer's instructions.

**Yield:  Slightly more than 1 quart**

*Variations:  For **Peanut Butter Chip Ice Cream**, add 3/4 cup of mini chocolate chips in final minutes of processing.*

*Note:  Use smooth OR crunchy peanut butter.

# Rocky Road
## Ice Cream

*This version of Rocky Road ice cream uses my two favorite nuts:  macadamias and walnuts.  Feel free to substitute an equal portion of YOUR favorite nuts.    Deb*

| | |
|---|---|
| 4 eggs yolks | 2 cups half and half |
| 3/4 cup sugar | 1/3 cup chopped walnuts |
| 1 tsp. vanilla extract | 1/3 cup chopped macadamia nuts |
| 1/2 cup cocoa powder | 2 oz. milk chocolate, chopped |
| 1 cup heavy cream | 1-7 oz. jar marshmallow creme |

In a large bowl, beat the egg yolks.  While continuing to beat, gradually add the sugar and vanilla.  Add the cocoa powder and blend well.  Finally, beat in the heavy cream and half and half.

Process in ice cream maker according to manufacturer's instructions.

Add the walnuts, macadamia nuts, and chocolate in final minutes of processing.

To pack:  In a 2 quart freezer container, alternate layers of ice cream with layers of marshmallow creme.

**Yield:  2 quarts**

# Key Lime
## Ice Cream

*If you think key limes make a wonderful pie, wait until you try this ice cream!*

| | |
|---|---|
| **5 egg yolks** | **1 cup heavy cream** |
| **1/3 cup sugar** | **1 cup half and half** |
| **1-14 oz. can condensed milk** | **Juice of 5 key limes\*** |

In a large bowl, beat the egg yolks. While continuing to beat, gradually add the sugar, condensed milk, heavy cream, and half and half. Add lime juice and mix well.

Process in ice cream maker according to manufacturer's instructions.

**Yield: 1 quart**

*Variations: For* **Margarita Ice Cream**, *add 1 Tbsp. of tequila AND 1 1/2 tsps. of triple sec in final minutes of processing.*

\*Note: You can substitute 1/2 cup of key lime juice concentrate.

# Orange
## Sherbet

*Fresh squeezed orange juice is the secret to this delicious sherbet.*

4 egg whites
1 cup superfine sugar
1 cup heavy cream

2 cups half and half
1 cup fresh orange juice (3-4 oranges)
Red and yellow food coloring (optional)

In a large bowl, beat the egg whites until frothy.  While continuing to beat, gradually add the sugar and beat until glossy.  Stir in the heavy cream, half and half, and orange juice.  Mix well.  If desired, color with drops of each food coloring to achieve a more intense orange hue.

Process in ice cream maker according to manufacturer's instructions.

**Yield:  Slightly more than 1 quart**

# Cantaloupe
## Ice Cream

*If you enjoy the sweet and smooth flavor of cantaloupe, you are sure to enjoy this recipe.  If you prefer pieces of fruit in your ice cream, add 1/2 cup of finely diced cantaloupe in the final minutes of processing.*

| | |
|---|---|
| 2 cups ripe cantaloupe, diced | 1 tsp. vanilla extract |
| 2 tsp. lime juice | 1 tsp. salt |
| 4 egg yolks | 2 cups heavy cream |
| 1 cup sugar | 1 cup half and half |

Combine the cantaloupe and lime juice in a blender and puree.  Chill until ready to use.  In a large mixing bowl, beat the egg yolks.  While continuing to beat, gradually add the sugar, vanilla, salt, heavy cream, and half and half.  Add the cantaloupe puree and blend well.

Process in ice cream maker according to manufacturer's instructions.

**Yield:  1 1/2 quarts**

# Honey Vanilla
## Ice Cream

*This ice cream is sweetened with honey. Some stores carry flavored honey such as cinnamon or lemon; these are a delicious substitute for traditional honey.*

**4 egg yolks**                    **¹/₂ cup honey**
**2 tsp. vanilla extract**         **2 cups heavy cream**
**Pinch of salt**                  **1 ¹/₂ cups half and half**

In a large bowl, beat the egg yolks. While continuing to beat, gradually add the vanilla, salt, honey, heavy cream, and half and half.

Process in ice cream maker according to manufacturer's instructions.

**Yield: Slightly more than 1 quart**

*Variations: For **Honey Vanilla Gelato**, use 3 ¹/₂ cups of milk in place of the cream and half and half.*

# Citrus
## Ice

*This sweet and tangy ice is refreshing!  Serve as a light dessert or as a palate cleanser between courses of a large meal.*

**2 cups grapefruit juice**
**1 cup pineapple juice**
**1 cup orange juice**
**1 cup cold water**
**1/3 cup + 1 Tbsp. honey**

In a blender or food processor, combine all of the ingredients.  Mix well.

Process in ice cream maker according to manufacturer's instructions.

**Yield:  Slightly more than 1 quart**

*Variations:  For <u>Honey Grapefruit Ice</u>, increase the quantity of grapefruit juice to 4 cups and the honey to 3/4 cup.  Eliminate the pineapple and orange juices.*

# Kiwi Delight
## Sherbet

*The kiwi is the key lime's new rival! Kiwi fruit makes a fabulously sweet, yet tangy, sherbet.*

**2 cups peeled and sliced kiwi fruit (about 6 kiwis)**
**1 cup sugar**
**2 Tbsp. orange juice**
**1 cup half and half**
**2 cups whole milk**

In a small saucepan, combine the kiwi, sugar, and orange juice. Cook over medium heat, uncovered, for 10 minutes. Stir occasionally. Let cool. In a blender or food processor, combine the cooled kiwi mixture, half and half, and milk. Mix well.

Process in ice cream maker according to manufacturer's instructions.

**Yield: Slightly more than 1 quart**

# Blackberry
## Sorbet

*This is a simple luscious dessert that is guaranteed to please almost any crowd.*

**2 cups fresh or frozen (defrosted) blackberries**
**1 cup sugar**
**3 Tbsp. orange juice**
**1 cup heavy cream**
**2 cups half and half**

In a small saucepan, combine the blackberries, sugar, and orange juice. Cook over medium heat, uncovered, for 10 minutes. Stir occasionally. Let cool. In a blender or food processor, combine the cooled blackberry mixture, heavy cream, and half and half. Mix well.

Process in ice cream maker according to manufacturer's instructions.

**Yield: 1 quart**

*Variations: For __Raspberry Sorbet__, substitute raspberries for the blackberries. For __Strawberry Sorbet__, substitute strawberries for the blackberries. For a __Mixed Berry Sorbet__, use a combination of blackberries, raspberries, and strawberries.*

# Apricot White Chocolate
## Ice Cream

*White chocolate is the perfect complement to the smooth texture of apricot. For the freshest apricot flavor, try making this recipe when they are in season.*

**4-5 fresh apricots (ripened, pitted, and halved), OR
1-16 oz. can of apricots, undrained
3 Tbsp. orange juice (use with fresh apricots only)
3 egg yolks
1 tsp. vanilla extract
1/2 cup sweetened condensed milk
1 1/2 cups half and half
1 cup grated premium white chocolate**

In a blender or food processor, puree the fresh apricots with orange juice OR the entire contents of the can of apricots. Add the remaining ingredients EXCEPT the white chocolate. Mix well.

Process in ice cream maker according to manufacturer's instructions.

Add the grated white chocolate in final minutes of processing.

**Yield: Slightly more than 1 quart**

# Ginger Plum
## Ice Cream

*By using canned plums, you can enjoy this unique combination of flavors all year long.  After all, ice cream is for all seasons!*

**2-16 oz. cans plums, juice reserved**
**1 tsp. powdered ginger**
**3 eggs**
**3/4 cup sugar**
**1 1/2 cups heavy cream**
**1 cup half and half**
**1/2 cup reserved plum juice**

Remove plums from cans and take out seeds.  In a blender or food processor, combine the plums, reserved juice, and remaining ingredients.  Mix well.  Strain mixture to eliminate plum skins and any seed pieces.

Process in ice cream maker according to manufacturer's instructions.

**Yield:  Slightly more than 1 quart**

# Watermelon
## Sorbet

*Capture the essence of summer with a cool and refreshing watermelon sorbet. It's a great way to indulge in a favorite summertime treat!*

> **2 cups watermelon, seeded and diced**
> **1/2 cup sugar**
> **2 Tbsp. orange juice**
> **1 cup half and half**
> **2 cups whole milk**

In a blender or food processor, combine all of the ingredients. Mix well.

Process in ice cream maker according to manufacturer's instructions.

**Yield: Slightly more than 1 quart**

# Peach
## Sherbet

*This is a real peach of a dessert! Enjoy this family favorite all year long by using fresh peaches in season and canned peaches when not in season.*

**2 cups fresh peaches (peeled, pitted, and sliced), OR
2 cups canned peaches, undrained
2 Tbsp. orange juice (use only with fresh peaches)
1/2 cup sugar
1 cup half and half
2 cups whole milk**

In a blender or food processor, combine all of the ingredients.  Mix well.

Process in ice cream maker according to manufacturer's instructions.

**Yield:  Slightly more than 1 quart**

# Island Delight
## Ice Cream

*The toasted coconut and macadamia nuts add a delightful crunchy texture to this ice cream. To toast the coconut, spread in a thin layer on a cookie sheet and bake in a 350 degree oven. Watch carefully, stirring every couple of minutes. Remove when the coconut is lightly browned.*

| | |
|---|---|
| 4 egg yolks | 1 cup toasted coconut (see above) |
| 1 cup sugar | 3/4 cup chopped macadamia nuts |
| 1 cup heavy cream | 1/8 cup rum |
| 1 3/4 cups half and half | |

In a large bowl, beat the egg yolks. While continuing to beat, gradually add the sugar, heavy cream, and half and half.

Process in ice cream maker according to manufacturer's instructions.

Add the coconut, macadamia nuts, and rum in final minutes of processing.

**Yield: Slightly more than 1 quart**

# Cream Soda
### Sherbet

*I'm not a big soda drinker, but I occasionally have a craving for an ice cold can of sweet cream soda. Needless to say, the soda somehow managed to find its way into my ice cream maker one day. Voilá - cream soda sherbet! Suzy*

**1-12 oz. can cream soda**
**1/2 cup sugar**
**1 cup half and half**
**2 cups whole milk**

In a blender or food processor, combine all of the ingredients. Mix well.

Process in ice cream maker according to manufacturer's instructions.

**Yield: Slightly more than 1 quart**

*Variations: For __Rootbeer Sherbet__, substitute a can of rootbeer for the cream soda.*

# Papaya
## Gelato

*If you've never had an Italian style gelato, this is a great recipe to start with.  It's simple to make and uses a fruit most of us don't take advantage of when in season.  Try serving this as a parfait, layered with whipped topping and diced papaya.*

**2 cups ripe papaya, diced**          **1 cup half and half**
**4 egg yolks**                        **1 cup milk**
**3/4 cup sugar**

Puree the papaya in a blender.  Add the remaining ingredients.  Mix well.

Process in ice cream maker according to manufacturer's instructions.

**Yield:  Slightly more than 1 quart**

*Variations:  For* **Mango Gelato**, *substitute 2 cups of diced mango for the papaya.*

# Sunset
## Gelato

*We call this a "sunset" gelato because it has the same pink-orange hue cast by the sun descending to the horizon. Try topping this with fresh whipped cream and a cherry and serving it to the kids as a Shirley Temple.*

**3 egg yolks**
**1/2 cup sweetened condensed milk**
**2 cups milk**

**3/4 cup mango nectar**
**3/4 cup apricot nectar**
**1/4 cup grenadine**

In a large bowl, beat the egg yolks. While continuing to beat, gradually add the condensed milk. Stir in the remaining ingredients. Mix well.

Process in ice cream maker according to manufacturer's instructions.

**Yield: 1 quart**

# Blueberry
## Ice Cream

*This ice cream can be made with fresh or frozen (defrosted) blueberries. If you can locate wild blueberries, you're in for a really special treat! We did not fuss with straining the puree and, as a result, the ice cream contained beautiful flecks of purple.*

2 cups blueberries
1 cup sugar
1 tsp. fresh orange zest
1 Tbsp. dark rum

1/4 tsp. nutmeg
3 egg yolks
2 cups heavy cream

Place the first 5 ingredients (blueberries through nutmeg) in a medium bowl and gently toss to coat the blueberries. Allow mixture to "marinate" in the refrigerator for 1-2 hours. Place the chilled blueberry mixture in a blender or food processor and puree. Add the egg yolks and heavy cream. Mix well.

Process in ice cream maker according to manufacturer's instructions.

**Yield: Slightly more than 1 quart**

# Suzy's "Your Choice"
## Ice Cream

*This recipe allows you to discover the basics of ice cream making. Start with the base recipe and add different ingredients. Let your imagination run wild and have fun!*

**3 eggs**                                 **2 cups heavy cream**
**3/4 cup sugar**                          **1 cup half and half**

In a blender or food processor, combine all of the ingredients. Mix well.

Process in ice cream maker according to manufacturer's instructions.

In final minutes of processing, add ***Your Choice*** of <u>ONE</u> of the following:

**1 cup mini chocolate chips or other candy pieces**
**1 cup of your favorite nuts, toasted if you like**
**1 cup shaved dark, milk, or white chocolate**
**1 cup of your favorite cookies, crumbled**
**1 cup of chopped brownie or fudge pieces**
**4-5 Tbsps. of your favorite liqueur**
**1/2 cup of your favorite coffee, brewed extra strong and cooled**

**Yield:  Slightly more than 1 quart**

**Pineapple Sherbet,** page 23

**Raspberry Mascarpone Ice Cream,** page 20

**Classic Strawberry Ice Cream,** page 9

Ice Cream to Go!

Cantaloupe Ice Cream, page 34

Pistachio Ice Cream, page 12

**Ginger Plum Ice Cream,** page 40

**Blueberry Ice Cream,** page 47

**Blackberry Sorbet,** page 38

**Honey Vanilla Ice Cream,** page 35

**Sunset Gelato,** page 46

**Mango Gelato,** page 45

**Papaya Gelato,** page 45

**Rum Raisin Ice Cream,** page 83

**Cannoli Ice Cream,** page 70

**Persimmon Ice Cream,** page 61

**Butterscotch Ice Cream,** page 65

**Chocolate Chip Cookie Dough Ice Cream,** page 57

**Fig Ice Cream,** page 69

**Fruitcake Ice Cream,** page 80

**Tiramisu Ice Cream,** page 81

**Vanilla Bean Ice Cream,** page 86

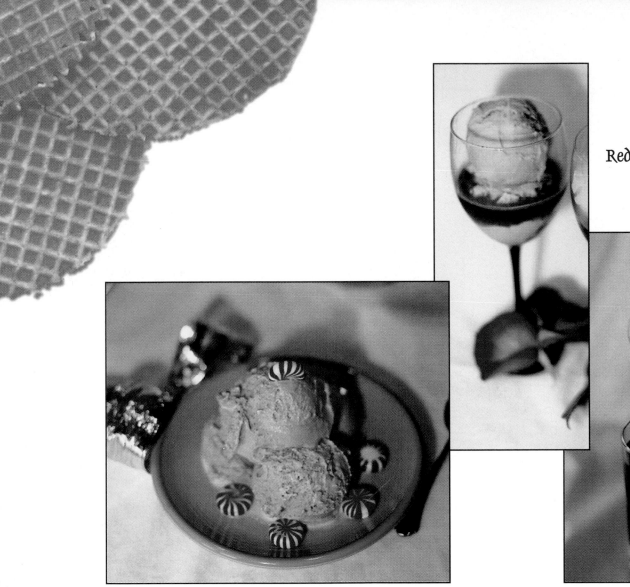

Red Wine Ice Cream, page 76

Peppermint Ice Cream, page 77

Grasshopper Ice Cream, page 84

# Fall

# Spiced Apple
## Ice Cream

*This is the ice cream version of apple pie.  Serve it alone topped with a warm caramel topping or on top of a hot slice of apple pie.*

| | |
|---|---|
| **1 1/2 cups canned apple pie filling** | **2 cups heavy cream** |
| **1 tsp. cinnamon** | **1 cup half and half** |
| **3 eggs** | **1 tsp. vanilla extract** |
| **3/4 cup sugar** | |

Remove apples from filling and coarsely chop.  Combine the apples with filling and cinnamon.  Set aside.  In a blender or food processor, combine the remaining ingredients.  Mix well.

Process in ice cream maker according to manufacturer's instructions.

Add the apple mixture in final minutes of processing.

**Yield:  Slightly more than 1 quart**

*Variations:  For __Apple Pie Ice Cream__, add 3/4 cup of graham cracker or vanilla wafer pieces in final minutes of processing.*

# Pumpkin Spice
## Ice Cream

*Since I've never been a big pumpkin pie fan, I was surprised that this recipe ended up being one of my favorites. It's a great finish to a cozy fall dinner.    Suzy*

**3 eggs**
**1 cup sugar**
**2 cups heavy cream**
**1 cup half and half**
**1 cup canned pumpkin (NOT pie filling)**

**1 tsp. vanilla extract**
**1/2 tsp. cinnamon**
**1/4 tsp. *each* ground ginger and nutmeg**
**1/8 tsp. cloves**

In a blender or food processor, combine all of the ingredients.  Mix well.

Process in ice cream maker according to manufacturer's instructions.

**Yield:  Slightly more than 1 quart**

*Variations:  For <u>Pumpkin Chip Ice Cream</u>, add 3/4 cup of mini chocolate chips in final minutes of processing.  For <u>Pumpkin Pie Ice Cream</u>, add 3/4 cup of graham cracker OR ginger snap pieces in final minutes of processing.*

# Cranberry
## Ice

*This ice makes a superb treat around the Thanksgiving and Christmas holidays. It has a beautiful speckled appearance and needs only a simple mint garnish. It also pairs nicely with delicate crisp cookies.*

**2 cups fresh cranberries**
**3 cups sugar**
**Juice of 1/2 lemon**

**3 cups cold water**
**1/2 cup light corn syrup**

In a blender or food processor, puree the first 3 ingredients (cranberries through lemon). Add the water and corn syrup. Mix well.

Process in ice cream maker according to manufacturer's instructions.

**Yield: 1 quart**

# Cider
## Ice

*This is a wonderful way to enjoy the fresh apple cider available from apple orchards or roadside stands in the fall.*

**1 1/4 cups sugar**
**1 1/4 cups cold water**
**1 3/4 cups fresh apple cider**

In a large saucepan, combine all of the ingredients.  Cook over medium heat, stirring constantly, until sugar dissolves.  Let cool.

Process in ice cream maker according to manufacturer's instructions.

**Yield:  Slightly less than 1 quart**

# Orange Spiced Tea
## Ice Cream

*This ice cream carries a hint of orange spice in each creamy scoop.  If you don't have orange spiced tea, experiment with other flavored teas.*

| | |
|---|---|
| 1 1/2 cups whole milk | 1 cup sugar |
| 2 orange spiced tea bags | 1 cup heavy cream |
| 4 egg yolks | 1 cup half and half |

In a small saucepan, heat the milk over medium heat.  Bring to a boil and remove from heat immediately.  Place the tea bags in a medium bowl and pour the heated milk over them.  Allow to steep for 5 minutes.

While the tea is steeping, beat the egg yolks in a large mixing bowl.  While continuing to beat, gradually add the sugar, heavy cream, and half and half.  Remove the tea bags from the warm milk.  Slowly add the milk to the cream mixture, while whisking constantly.  Transfer the mixture to a large saucepan and cook over medium heat, stirring constantly, for 10-12 minutes.  DO NOT boil.  Chill in the refrigerator tightly covered with plastic wrap.

Process in ice cream maker according to manufacturer's instructions.

**Yield:  1 1/2 quarts**

# Pecan Praline
## Ice Cream

*As an uprooted New Orleanian, I enjoy thinking of my childhood as I make this nostalgic recipe.  I grew up eating pralines - creamy, sugary, pecan confections that are to die for!  Adding a similar concoction to a praline flavored ice cream produces a sinfully rich ice cream.    Suzy*

3 eggs
3/4 cup sugar
2 cups heavy cream

1 cup half and half
2 Tbsp. praline flavored coffee syrup
2 cups Praline Pecans (recipe follows)

Make Praline Pecans first!

In a blender or food processor, combine all of the ingredients EXCEPT the praline pecans.  Mix well.

Process in ice cream maker according to manufacturer's instructions.

Add the Praline Pecans in final minutes of processing.

**Yield:  Slightly more than 1 quart**

**Praline Pecans:  Boil 1 cup butter and 1 cup brown sugar for 2 minutes.  Add pecans, stirring to thoroughly coat.  Remove from heat and let cool.  Makes about 3 1/2 cups.  (This is also delicious as an ice cream topping!)**

# Chocolate Chip Cookie Dough
## Ice Cream

*Use your own homemade cookie dough or save time by using the pre-made chocolate chip cookie dough that is sold in the refrigerator section of most supermarkets.  This is a favorite with kids!*

| | |
|---|---|
| **4 egg yolks** | **2 cups half and half** |
| **1 cup sugar** | **1/2 cup grated chocolate** |
| **2 tsp. vanilla extract** | **1 1/2 cups chocolate chip cookie dough** |
| **1 cup heavy cream** | **(broken into small pieces and chilled)** |

In a large bowl, beat the egg yolks.  While continuing to beat, gradually add the sugar, vanilla, heavy cream, and half and half.

Process in ice cream maker according to manufacturer's instructions.

Add the grated chocolate and cookie dough pieces in final minutes of processing.

**Yield:  Slightly more than 1 quart**

# Spice
## Ice Cream

*The secret to this incredible ice cream is toasting the spices.  Toasting intensifies the flavors and leaves your kitchen smelling irresistable.*

| | |
|---|---|
| **1 Tbsp. cinnamon** | **1 cup sugar** |
| **1 Tbsp. nutmeg** | **1 cup heavy cream** |
| **1 Tbsp. allspice** | **2 1/2 cups half and half** |
| **3 eggs** | |

Toast the first 3 ingredients by spreading in a thin layer on a cookie sheet and baking in a 350 degree oven for 2-3 minutes.  Watch carefully to avoid scorching.  Let cool.

In a large bowl, beat the eggs.  While continuing to beat, gradually add the sugar, heavy cream, and half and half.  Finally, blend in the toasted spices.

Process in ice cream maker according to manufacturer's instructions.

**Yield:  1 1/2 quarts**

*Variations:  For <u>Walnut Spice Ice Cream</u>, add 1 cup of chopped walnuts in final minutes of processing.  For <u>Chocolate Spice Ice Cream</u>, add 1 cup of mini chocolate chips in final minutes of processing.  For <u>Spiced Cookie Dough Ice Cream</u>, add 1 cup of crumbled oatmeal raisin cookie dough in final minutes of processing.*

# Gingered Pear
## Sorbet

*Ginger coupled with pears creates a warm and unique blend of flavors in this delectable sorbet.*

**3-4 large red pears (peeled, cored, and diced)**
**1 1/4 cups water**
**Juice of 1/2 lime**
**2 Tbsp. candied ginger, coarsely chopped**
**1 1/2 cups sugar**
**1 cup heavy cream**

In a large saucepan, cook the pears, water, lime juice, and ginger over medium heat until the pears are tender. Puree the pear mixture in a blender or food processor. Return the mixture to the saucepan and add the sugar. Cook over medium heat for 2-3 minutes, stirring frequently, until the sugar dissolves. Place the mixture in the refrigerator and chill well. Add the heavy cream to the chilled pear mixture and mix well.

Process in ice cream maker according to manufacturer's instructions.

**Yield:** **1 1/2 quarts**

*Variations: For* **Apple Cinnamon Sorbet**, *substitute 4 to 5 baking apples for the pears and 2 tsp. of ground cinnamon for the candied ginger.*

# Orange Cream with Spiced Pecans
### Ice Cream

*The nuts can be made ahead of time and frozen until ready for use. These nuts are so good that we often make a double batch and use the leftover halves for snacking or as an ice cream topping.*

| | |
|---|---|
| 1 egg white | 4 egg yolks |
| 1 Tbsp. bourbon | 1 cup sugar |
| 1/4 tsp. salt | 1 cup heavy cream |
| 1/2 tsp. cinnamon | 1 cup half and half |
| 2 Tbsp. sugar | 1 cup orange juice concentrate, thawed |
| 3 cups pecan halves | |

In a large bowl, beat the egg white until frothy. Stir in the bourbon, salt, cinnamon, and sugar. Fold pecans into the mixture and coat well. Spread in single layer on a cookie sheet. Bake in a 225 degree oven for approximately 1 hour, stirring every 15 minutes. Cool and break apart. Set aside. In another large bowl, beat the egg yolks. While continuing to beat, gradually add the sugar, heavy cream, and half and half. Add orange juice concentrate. Mix well.

Process in ice cream maker according to manufacturer's instructions.

Add **1 CUP** of the pecans in final minutes of processing.

**Yield: 1 1/2 quarts**

# Persimmon
## Ice Cream

*Persimmons have a wonderful earthy flavor characteristic of the fall season. Choose fruit that has a deep orange-red flesh. Ripen the fruit by placing in a brown paper bag and letting sit at room temperature for a few days. Check the fruit daily for softness. Although the skins are edible, peel the fruit for this recipe.*

**2 cups fresh persimmon, peeled and diced (4-5 persimmons)**

| | |
|---|---|
| **1/2 tsp. allspice** | **4 egg yolks** |
| **3 Tbsp. brown sugar** | **3/4 cup sugar** |
| **Pinch of salt** | **2 cups heavy cream** |

In a large saucepan, combine the persimmon, allspice, brown sugar, and salt. Cook over low-medium heat until the fruit is very soft. Transfer the cooked fruit mixture to a blender or food processor and puree. Let cool. Add the remaining ingredients and mix well.

Process in ice cream maker according to manufacturer's instructions.

**Yield: Slightly more than 1 1/2 quarts**

*Variations: For **Butternut Squash Ice Cream**, substitute diced butternut squash for the persimmon.*

# Cinnamon Stick
## Ice Cream

*Whip up this delicious and simple to make ice cream anytime.  It's the perfect accompaniment to a variety of pies; skip plain old vanilla and create your own special á la mode desserts.*

| | |
|---|---|
| 1 Tbsp. ground cinnamon, toasted | 2 cups heavy cream |
| 3 eggs | 1 cup half and half |
| 3/4 cup sugar | 1 tsp. vanilla extract |

Toast the cinnamon by spreading in a thin layer on a cookie sheet and baking in a 350 degree oven for 5-8 minutes.  Shake pan during baking and watch carefully to avoid scorching.  Let cool.

In a blender or food processor, combine all of the ingredients.  Mix well.

Process in ice cream maker according to manufacturer's instructions.

**Yield:  1 quart**

# Butter Pecan
## Ice Cream

*The secret to this recipe is the salty toasted pecans and lots of them!*

| | |
|---|---|
| 1 egg white | 3/4 cup sugar |
| 1 tsp. salt, divided | 2 cups heavy cream |
| 3 eggs | 1 cup half and half |
| 1 1/2 cups pecan pieces | 1/2 stick butter, melted and cooled (cool at room temperature) |

Whisk the egg white and 1/2 tsp. of salt together until frothy. Fold the pecans into the mixture and coat well. Toast the pecans by spreading in a single layer on a cookie sheet and baking in a 350 degree oven for approximately 10 minutes. Stir once halfway through cooking. Let cool.

In a blender or food processor, combine the remaining ingredients EXCEPT the pecans. Mix well.

Process in ice cream maker according to manufacturer's instructions.

Add the pecans in final minutes of processing.

**Yield: Slightly more than 1 quart**

*Variations: For __Butter Almond Ice Cream__, substitute 1 1/2 cups of almonds for the pecans.*

# Toasted Almond
## Ice Cream

*Toasting the almonds in this recipe imparts a wonderful and uniquely flavorful crunch to the ice cream.*

| | |
|---|---|
| 1 cup whole almonds, toasted | 2 cups heavy cream |
| 3 eggs | 1 cup half and half |
| 3/4 cup sugar | 1 Tbsp. almond extract |

Toast the almonds by spreading in a single layer on a cookie sheet and baking in a 350 degree oven for approximately 10 minutes.  Stir once halfway through cooking.  Watch carefully to avoid scorching.  Let cool.  (If you desire, you may coarsley chop the almonds.)

In a blender or food processor, combine all of the remaining ingredients EXCEPT the almonds.  Mix well.

Process in ice cream maker according to manufacturer's instructions.

Add the almonds in final minutes of processing.

**Yield:  Slightly more than 1 quart**

# Butterscotch
## Ice Cream

*I was inspired to create this ice cream while walking the candy aisle in the supermarket. Using real butterscotch candy gives the ice cream a fabulous flavor, not to mention a lovely soft buttery color. Suzy*

**3/4 cup crushed butterscotch candies (1-6.5 oz. package)**
**3/4 cup sugar**
**3 eggs**
**2 cups heavy cream**
**1 cup half and half**

Crush the candies by placing inside a plastic bag and pounding with a rolling pin.

In a blender or food processor, combine all of the ingredients including the crushed candy. Mix well.

Process in ice cream maker according to manufacturer's instructions.

**Yield: Slightly more than 1 quart**

*Variations: For <u>Rootbeer Ice Cream</u>, substitute rootbeer candies for the butterscotch candies.*

# Cappucino
## Gelato

*This gelato is a must for coffee lovers like us!*

**2 eggs**
**1 cup sugar**
**2 tsp. vanilla extract**

**2 1/2 cups milk**
**1-10 oz. can cappucino drink**

In a large bowl, beat the eggs.  While continuing to beat, gradually add the sugar and vanilla.  Add the milk and cappucino drink.  Mix well.

Process in ice cream maker according to manufacturer's instructions.

**Yield:  1 quart**

*Variations:  For __Flavored Cappucino Gelato__, add 2 Tbsp. of a flavored syrup when adding milk and cappucino drink.  For __Mocha Cappucino Gelato__, add 1 cup of shaved chocolate in final minutes of processing.*

# Cranberry Raspberry
## Sorbet

*This sorbet is light, refreshing, and very simple to make.*

| | |
|---|---|
| **3 egg whites** | **2 tsp. fresh orange zest or 1 tsp. dried** |
| **1 cup sugar** | **2 Tbsp. lemon juice** |
| **1 can cranberry raspberry sauce*** | **1 cup half and half** |

In a large bowl, beat the egg whites until frothy.  While continuing to beat, gradually add the sugar.  Beat until soft shiny peaks form.  In a separate large bowl, combine the sauce, orange zest, lemon juice, and half and half. Mix well.  Fold in the egg white mixture.

Process in ice cream maker according to manufacturer's instructions.

**Yield:  1 quart**

*Variations:  For __Cranberry Sorbet__, substitute regular canned cranberry sauce for the cranberry raspberry sauce.*

*This sauce can be found where you find traditional canned cranberry sauce.

# Pumpkin Cheesecake
## Ice Cream

*This recipe is an excellent alternative to a traditional holiday pumpkin pie dessert. It's a rich, elegant, ice cream that is simple to make. Serve with a good cup of coffee for a fabulous ending to a great holiday meal.*

1 cup sugar
1 tsp. vanilla extract
1/2 tsp. cinnamon
1/4 tsp. *each* ginger and nutmeg
1/8 tsp. cloves

3 eggs
2 cups heavy cream
1/2 cup half and half
8 oz. cream cheese, softened
3/4 cup canned pumpkin
(NOT pie filling)

In a blender or food processor, combine all of the ingredients. Mix well.

Process in ice cream maker according to manufacturer's instructions.

**Yield: Slightly more than 1 quart**

# Fig
## Ice Cream

*This recipe is for my mother. While discussing ice cream flavors, she mentioned that she'd once had an incredible fresh fig ice cream. Since I couldn't readily obtain fresh figs, I thought I'd try to create something with dried figs. The result was positively spectacular! This fig ice cream is very rich and intensely flavored. Suzy*

**9 oz. package dried figs**
**1/3 cup orange juice**
**1 tsp. vanilla extract**
**3 eggs**

**3/4 cup sugar**
**2 cups heavy cream**
**1 cup half and half**

Cut stems off of the dried figs. In a small saucepan, combine the figs, orange juice, and vanilla. Simmer on low heat, uncovered, for 15 minutes. Let cool. Run fig mixture through a food mill, yielding approximately 3/4 cup of fig puree.

In a blender or food processor, combine the fig puree and remaining ingredients. Mix well.

Process in ice cream maker according to manufacturer's instructions.

**Yield: Slightly more than 1 quart**

# Cannoli
## Ice Cream

*If you like the traditional Italian pastry cannoli, you'll love this ice cream!*

**3 eggs**
**3/4 cup sugar**
**2 cups heavy cream**
**1 cup half and half**

**8 oz. ricotta cheese**
**3/4 cup pistachios, shelled and chopped**
**1/2 cup candied cherries, chopped**

In a blender or food processor, combine the first 5 ingredients (eggs through ricotta cheese).  Mix well.

Process in ice cream maker according to manufacturer's instructions.

Add the pistachios and cherries in final minutes of processing.

**Yield:  Slightly more than 1 quart**

*Variations:  For __Cannoli Chip Ice Cream__, substitute 3/4 cup of mini chocolate chips for the cherries.*

# Winter

# Kiss Me Again Chocolate
## Ice Cream

*This ice cream is reminiscent of chocolate mousse: a perfect Valentine's Day treat! We added a combination of finely grated white and dark chocolate for an unimposing effect. If you prefer more texture, use coarsely chopped chocolate instead of the grated.*

| | |
|---|---|
| **4 egg yolks** | **1 cup heavy cream** |
| **1 cup sugar** | **1 1/2 cups half and half** |
| **1/2 cup cocoa powder** | **1 cup finely grated chocolate** |
| **1 tsp. vanilla extract** | |

In a large bowl, beat the egg yolks. While continuing to beat, gradually add the sugar. Add the cocoa powder and vanilla. Blend well. Finally, beat in the heavy cream and half and half.

Process in ice cream maker according to manufacturer's instructions.

Add the grated chocolate in final minutes of processing.

**Yield:  Slightly more than 1 quart**

# Mint Chocolate Chip
## Ice Cream

*No ice cream book is complete without a recipe for this classic flavor!*

3 eggs
3/4 cup sugar
2 cups heavy cream
1 cup half and half

3/4 tsp. peppermint extract
6-7 drops green food coloring (optional)
3/4 cup mini chocolate chips

In a blender or food processor, combine all of the ingredients EXCEPT the chocolate chips.  Mix well.

Process in ice cream maker according to manufacturer's instructions.

Add the chocolate chips in final minutes of processing.

**Yield:  Slightly more than 1 quart**

*Variations:  For __Mint Dark Chocolate Ice Cream__, substitute 3/4 cup of shaved dark chocolate for the chocolate chips.  For __Mint Almond Ice Cream__, substitute 3/4 cup of (toasted) almonds for the chocolate chips.*

# Mimosa
## Ice

*This ice is an excellent accompaniment to brunch.  Serve as an ice or let the ice defrost a little and serve as a slushy drink in champagne glasses.  It adds the perfect festive touch.*

**3 cups *good quality* champagne**
**2 cups orange juice**

Combine the champagne and orange juice in the ice cream maker and process according to manufacturer's instructions.

**Yield:  Slightly more than 1 quart**

# Red Wine
## Ice Cream

*This ice cream flavor was inspired by our love for the reds.  Choose a good quality wine that you enjoy and you are sure to relish each bite of this frozen treat.*

| | |
|---|---|
| **3 eggs** | **1 cup half and half** |
| **3/4 cup sugar** | **1 cup red wine** |
| **1 1/2 cups heavy cream** | |

Chill the red wine until ready for use.  In a large bowl, beat the eggs.  While continuing to beat, gradually add the sugar, heavy cream, and half and half.  Add chilled red wine and mix well.

Process in ice cream maker according to manufacturer's instructions.

**Yield:  Slightly more than 1 quart**

*Variations:  For <u>Port Wine Ice Cream</u>, substitute 1/2 cup of chilled port wine for the red wine.  Also, increase the half and half to 1 1/2 cups.*

# Peppermint
## Ice Cream

*This ice cream is a perfect Christmastime treat.  Enjoy it alone or drizzled with chocolate sauce.*

| | |
|---|---|
| **3/4 cup crushed peppermint candies** | **1 cup half and half** |
| **3/4 cup sugar** | **3 eggs** |
| **2 cups heavy cream** | **5-6 drops red food coloring (optional)** |

Crush candies by placing inside a plastic bag and pounding with a rolling pin.

In a blender or food processor, combine all of the ingredients including the crushed candies.  Mix well.

Process in ice cream maker according to manufacturer's instructions.

**Yield:  Slightly more than 1 quart**

*Variations:  For <u>Spearmint Ice Cream</u>, substitute green spearmint candies for the peppermints and use green food coloring instead of red.*

# White Chocolate Cherry
### Ice Cream

*Serve this ice cream around the Christmas holidays; the red and green cherries look very festive.*

**4 oz. white chocolate bar, melted**
**3 eggs**
**3/4 cup sugar**

**2 cups heavy cream**
**1 cup half and half**
**1-10 oz. jar cherries, drained**
**(use red, green, or a combination)**

Melt chocolate over double boiler or in microwave.  Let cool at room temperature.

In a blender or food processor, combine the cooled chocolate with all of the remaining ingredients EXCEPT the cherries.

Process in ice cream maker according to manufacturer's instructions.

Add the cherries in final minutes of processing.

**Yield:  Slightly more than 1 quart**

*Variations:  For **White Chocolate Nut Ice Cream**, substitute 1 cup of (toasted) nuts for the cherries.*

# Egg Nog
## Ice Cream

*This is a fabulous way to enjoy your holiday egg nog.  Keep a batch in the freezer around the holidays for those unexpected visitors.*

| | |
|---|---|
| **4 eggs, separated** | **2 cups heavy cream** |
| **1 cup powdered sugar** | **1 tsp. nutmeg** |
| **2 tsp. vanilla extract** | **1/8 cup brandy OR bourbon** |

In a small bowl, beat the egg whites until stiff.  Set aside.  In a separate large bowl, beat the egg yolks until creamy.  Add the powdered sugar and vanilla; blend well.  Beat in the heavy cream and nutmeg.  Fold in egg whites.

Process in ice cream maker according to manufacturer's instructions.

Add the brandy OR bourbon in final minutes of processing.

**Yield:  1 1/2 quarts**

*Variations:  For a "Quick" Egg Nog Ice Cream, substitute 4 cups of ready made egg nog for the **FIRST 4** ingredients.*

# Fruitcake
## Ice Cream

*My mother makes fruitcake every year for gift giving.  With an abundance of fruitcake ingredients available around the holidays, I saw an opportunity to blend a holiday tradition with a favorite dessert!    Deb*

| | |
|---|---|
| 1 cup fruit cake mix candied fruit | 1 cup sugar |
| 3 Tbsp. brandy | 1 Tbsp. molasses |
| 1 cup half and half | 2 cups heavy cream |
| 1 slice wheat bread, crust removed | 1/2 cup chopped walnuts |
| 4 egg yolks | |

In a small bowl, combine the candied fruit and brandy.  Set aside.  In a separate shallow bowl, soak the bread in the half and half for 10-15 minutes.  Once the bread is soggy, blend until smooth and the bread is evenly dispersed in half and half.  In a large bowl, beat the egg yolks.  While continuing to beat, gradually add the sugar, molasses, heavy cream, and half and half/bread mixture.

Process in ice cream maker according to manufacturer's instructions.

Add the candied fruit mixture AND walnuts in final minutes of processing.

**Yield:  Slightly more than 1 quart**

# Tiramisu
## Ice Cream

*When dining at our favorite Italian restaurant, we always look forward to the grand finale - tiramisu. This frozen version is equally enjoyable and, since it can be stored in the freezer, it can be enjoyed for days.*

3 Tbsp. sugar
1/2 cup brewed espresso coffee, hot
1/8 cup brandy
8-10 ladyfinger cookies
4 egg yolks

2/3 cup sugar
8 oz. mascarpone cheese
1 cup heavy cream
1 cup half and half

Combine 3 Tbsps. sugar, espresso, and brandy to make a syrup. Stir well. Place ladyfingers on a small cookie sheet and brush with some of the syrup; refrigerate until ready for use. Reserve remaining espresso syrup.

In a large bowl, beat the egg yolks. While continuing to beat, gradually add the sugar and 2 Tbsp. of the reserved espresso syrup. Beat in the mascarpone cheese, heavy cream, and half and half.

Process in ice cream maker according to manufacturer's instructions.

While the ice cream is processing, crumble the chilled ladyfingers. Add the crumbled ladyfingers and remaining espresso syrup in final minutes of processing.

**Yield: Slightly more than 1 quart**

# White Chocolate Macadamia Nut
### Ice Cream

*These two delicate flavors combine very nicely. Serve on a cocoa dusted plate or drizzled with a sweetened raspberry puree.*

**4 oz. white chocolate bar, melted**
**3 eggs**
**3/4 cup sugar**

**2 cups heavy cream**
**1 cup half and half**
**3/4 cup chopped macadamia nuts**
**(1-3.25 oz. jar)**

Melt chocolate over double boiler or in microwave. Let cool at room temperature.

In a blender or food processor, combine the cooled chocolate with the remaining ingredients EXCEPT macadamia nuts. Mix well.

Process in ice cream maker according to manufacturer's instructions.

Add the macadamia nuts in final minutes of processing.

**Yield: Slightly more than 1 quart**

*Variations: For __White Chocolate Almond Ice Cream__, substitute toasted almonds for the macadamia nuts.*

# Rum Raisin
## Ice Cream

*This old favorite is the perfect treat to enjoy in the depths of winter while curled up by the fireplace.*

| | |
|---|---|
| 1 cup raisins | 2 cups heavy cream |
| 3/4 cup rum | 1 cup half and half |
| 3 eggs | 1 tsp. vanilla extract |
| 3/4 cup sugar | |

In a small saucepan, simmer the raisins in the rum, stirring occasionally. Simmer approximately 10 minutes or until the raisins plump and are somewhat soft. Strain the raisins. Reserve the liquid and let both cool.

In a blender or food processor, combine the cooled rum/raisin liquid with the remaining ingredients EXCEPT raisins. Mix well.

Process in ice cream maker according to manufacturer's instructions.

Add the raisins in final minutes of processing.

**Yield: Slightly more than 1 quart**

# Grasshopper
## Ice Cream

*This is the ice cream version of the classic after dinner drink.  Serve this with a drizzle of chocolate syrup, a dollop of whipped cream, and a garnish of fresh mint sprigs.*

| | |
|---|---|
| 4 egg yolks | 1 1/2 cups half and half |
| 1 cup sugar | 3 Tbsp. creme de menthe |
| 1 1/2 cups heavy cream | 1 Tbsp. creme de cocoa |

In a large bowl, beat the egg yolks.  While continuing to beat, gradually add the sugar, heavy cream, and half and half.

Process in ice cream maker according to manufacturer's instructions.

Add the creme de menthe and creme de cocoa in final minutes of processing.

**Yield:  1 quart**

# Mocha
## Ice Cream

*Coffee lovers and chocolate lovers alike can't resist this wonderful duo of flavors.  For a fancy dessert, serve the ice cream drizzled with your favorite coffee or chocolate flavored liqueur.*

**3 eggs**
**3/4 cup sugar**
**2 cups heavy cream**

**1 cup half and half**
**1/2 cup strongly brewed coffee, cooled**
**1/3 heaping cup of cocoa powder**

In a blender or food processor, combine all of the ingredients.  Mix well.

Process in ice cream maker according to manufacturer's instructions.

**Yield:  Slightly more than 1 quart**

*Variations:  For* **Mocha Chip Ice Cream**, *add 3/4 cup of mini chocolate chips in final minutes of processing.*

# Vanilla Bean
### Ice Cream

*The first homemade ice cream I ever tasted was vanilla bean and the memory is still quite clear to this day.  The flavor of a fresh vanilla bean is unequalled.    Deb*

**2 cups half and half**                    **1 cup sugar**
**1 vanilla bean, split**                    **2 cups heavy cream**
**4 egg yolks**

Pour half and half into a large saucepan.  Scrape the seeds from the vanilla bean and add to the half and half along with the bean.  Simmer over low heat for 12-15 minutes, stirring occasionally.   Remove from heat and discard the bean.

In a large bowl, beat the egg yolks.  While continuing to beat, gradually add the sugar, heavy cream, and vanilla flavored half and half.  Return the mixture to the saucepan and increase heat to medium.  Cook for 8-10 minutes, stirring constantly.  DO NOT boil.  Chill mixture in refrigerator, tightly covered with plastic wrap.

Process in ice cream maker according to manufacturer's instructions.

**Yield:  Slightly more than 1 quart**

# Amaretto
## Ice Cream

*This is a versatile ice cream that can be served as a dessert drizzled with a little additional liqueur or served softened in a stem glass as an after dinner drink.*

| | |
|---|---|
| 3 eggs | 1 cup half and half |
| 3/4 cup sugar | 1 tsp. vanilla extract |
| 2 cups heavy cream | 5-6 Tbsp. Amaretto liqueur |

In a blender or food processor, combine all of the ingredients.  Mix well.

Process in ice cream maker according to manufacturer's instructions.

**Yield:  Slightly more than 1 quart**

*Variations:  For* **Hazelnut Ice Cream**, *substitute Hazelnut liqueur for the Amaretto.*

# Red Currant
## Ice Cream

*This recipe was designed as a simple way to impart the flavor of red currants without the fuss of finding and preparing the fruit.  Almost any flavor jelly works; keep an eye open for interesting flavors in the jelly section of your supermarket.*

| | |
|---|---|
| **1 cup red currant jelly** | **2 1/2 cups half and half** |
| **3 egg yolks** | **1 tsp. vanilla extract** |
| **1 cup heavy cream** | |

In a small saucepan, over low heat, melt the jelly.  Set aside.

In a large bowl, beat the egg yolks.  While continuing to beat, gradually add the heavy cream, half and half, and vanilla.  Place the cream mixture in a large saucepan and cook over medium heat for 10-12 minutes, stirring constantly.  Remove from heat and whisk in the melted jelly.  Place the mixture in the refrigerator, covered tightly with plastic wrap, until well chilled.

Process in ice cream maker according to manufacturer's instructions.

**Yield:  1 quart**

# Triple Chocolate Overload
## Ice Cream

*This recipe is a must for the true chocoholic!*

3 eggs
3/4 cup sugar
2 cups heavy cream
1 cup half and half

1/3 cup cocoa powder
1/2 cup chocolate chips
3/4 cup fudge or brownie pieces
(make your own or use store bought)

In a blender or food processor, combine all of the ingredients EXCEPT chocolate chips and fudge or brownie pieces. Mix well.

Process in ice cream maker according to manufacturer's instructions.

Add the chocolate chips and fudge or brownie pieces in final minutes of processing.

**Yield: Slightly more than 1 quart**

# Green Tea
## Ice Cream

*This ice cream is the perfect finale to an Asian feast.*

| | |
|---|---|
| 1 1/2 cups half and half | 1 1/4 cups sugar |
| 4 green tea bags | 1 1/4 cups heavy cream |
| 4 egg yolks | |

In a small saucepan, heat the half and half over medium heat. Bring to a boil and remove from heat immediately. Place the tea bags in a medium bowl and pour the heated half and half over them. Allow to steep for 5 minutes.

While the tea is steeping, beat the egg yolks in a large mixing bowl. While continuing to beat, gradually add the sugar and heavy cream. Remove the tea bags from the warm half and half. Slowly add the half and half to the cream mixture, while whisking constantly. Transfer the mixture to a large saucepan and cook over medium heat, stirring constantly, for 10-12 minutes. DO NOT boil. Chill in the refrigerator tightly covered with plastic wrap.

Process in ice cream maker according to manufacturer's instructions.

**Yield:  1 quart**

# Deb's "Your Choice"
## Ice Cream

*When it comes to ice cream creations, the possibilities are endless. This recipe is designed for you; it is your opportunity to experiment with your favorite flavor or blend of flavors. Have fun!*

| | |
|---|---|
| **3 egg yolks** | **1 cup heavy cream** |
| **1 cup sugar** | **2 cups half and half** |

In a large bowl, beat the egg yolks. While continuing to beat, gradually add the sugar, heavy cream, and half and half. Transfer to a large saucepan and cook over medium heat, stirring constantly, for 10-12 minutes. DO NOT boil. Chill in the refrigerator, tightly covered with plastic wrap.

**Prior** to processing, add *Your Choice* of ONE of the following: 2 Tbsp. of your favorite spice or spice blend, 1 cup of thawed fruit juice concentrate, 3 Tbsp. of flavored coffee syrup, 1 cup of your favorite fruit puree, 1-3.4 oz. package of powdered pudding mix, or your favorite extract flavoring, to taste. Mix well.

Process in ice cream maker according to manufacturer's instructions.

**Instead** of adding an ingredient prior to processing, add *Your Choice* of ONE of the following in the final minutes of processing: 1 cup of cookie dough pieces, 1 cup of your favorite nuts (toasted, sugared, or spiced), 1 cup of diced fruit, 1 cup of your favorite candy bar pieces, or 1/8 cup of liqueur.

**Yield: Slightly more than 1 quart**

# Dark Chocolate Cheesecake
## Ice Cream

*If you like the intensity of dark chocolate, you'll love the richness of it combined with cream cheese in this dense delicious ice cream.*

| | |
|---|---|
| 3 oz. dark chocolate bar, melted | 2 cups heavy cream |
| 3 eggs | 1 cup half and half |
| 3/4 cup sugar | 8 oz. cream cheese, softened |

Melt chocolate over double boiler or in microwave.  Let cool at room temperature.

In a blender or food processor, combine all of the ingredients including melted chocolate.  Mix well.

Process in ice cream maker according to manufacturer's instructions.

**Yield:  Slightly more than 1 quart**

# Recipe Index

Almond Coconut Candy Bar Ice Cream, 26
Amaretto Ice Cream, 87
Apple Cinnamon Sorbet, 59
Apple Pie Ice Cream, 51
Apricot White Chocolate Ice Cream, 39

Banana Chocolate Chip Ice Cream, 29
Banana Dream Ice Cream, 29
Banana Nut Ice Cream, 29
Blackberry Sorbet, 38
Blueberry Ice, 19
Blueberry Ice Cream, 47
Butter Almond Ice Cream, 63
Butter Pecan Ice Cream, 63
Butternut Squash Ice Cream, 61
Butterscotch Ice Cream, 65

Cannoli Chip Ice Cream, 70
Cannoli Ice Cream, 70
Cantaloupe Ice Cream, 34
Cappucino Gelato, 66
Cherry Sherbet, 24
Chocolate
        Apricot White Chocolate Ice
        Cream, 39

Banana Chocolate Chip Ice
        Cream, 29
Cannoli Chip Ice Cream, 70
Chocolate Cherry Sherbet, 24
Chocolate Chip Cookie Dough Ice
        Cream, 57
Chocolate Spice Ice Cream, 58
Chocolate Walnut Ice Cream, 8
Classic Chocolate Ice Cream, 8
Double Chocolate Walnut Ice
        Cream, 8
Kiss Me Again Chocolate Ice
        Cream, 73
Mint Chocolate Chip Ice
        Cream, 74
Mint Dark Chocolate Ice
        Cream, 74
Mocha Chip Ice Cream, 85
Peanut Butter Chip Ice Cream, 30
Pumpkin Chip Ice Cream, 52
Raspberry Truffle Ice Cream, 20
Rocky Road Ice Cream, 31
Spumoni Ice Cream, 10
Strawberry Chocolate Chip Ice
        Cream, 9

Triple Chocolate Overload Ice
        Cream, 89
White Chocolate Almond Ice
        Cream, 82
White Chocolate Cherry Ice
        Cream, 78
White Chocolate Macadamia Nut
        Ice Cream, 82
White Chocolate Nut Ice
        Cream, 78
Chocolate Cherry Sherbet, 24
Chocolate Chip Cookie Dough Ice Cream, 57
Chocolate Spice Ice Cream, 58
Chocolate Walnut Ice Cream, 8
Cider Ice, 54
Cinnamon Stick Ice Cream, 62
Citrus Ice, 36
Classic Chocolate Ice Cream, 8
Classic Strawberry Ice Cream, 9
Classic Vanilla Ice Cream, 7
Coconut Candy Bar Ice Cream, 26
Coconut Ice Cream, 14
Cranberry Ice, 53
Cranberry Raspberry Sorbet, 67
Cranberry Sorbet, 67

Cream Soda Sherbet, 44

Dark Chocolate Cheesecake Ice Cream, 92
Deb's Your Choice Ice Cream, 91
Double Chocolate Walnut Ice Cream, 8
Double Coconut Ice Cream, 14

Eggnog Ice Cream, 79

Fig Ice Cream, 69
Flavored Cappucino Gelato, 66
Fruitcake Ice Cream, 80

Gelatos
    Cappucino, 66
    Flavored Cappucino, 66
    Honey Vanilla, 35
    Mango, 45
    Mocha Cappucino, 66
    Papaya, 45
    Sunset, 46
Ginger Peach Ice Cream, 25
Ginger Plum Ice Cream, 40
Gingered Pear Sorbet, 59
Grasshopper Ice Cream, 84
Green Tea Ice Cream, 90

Hazelnut Ice Cream, 87

Honey Grapefruit Ice, 36
Honey Vanilla Gelato, 35
Honey Vanilla Ice Cream, 35

Ice Creams
    Almond Coconut Candy Bar, 26
    Amaretto, 87
    Apple Pie, 51
    Apricot White Chocolate, 39
    Banana Chocolate Chip Ice
        Cream, 29
    Banana Dream, 29
    Banana Nut, 29
    Blueberry, 47
    Butter Almond, 63
    Butter Pecan, 63
    Butternut Squash, 61
    Butterscotch, 65
    Cannoli, 70
    Cannoli Chip, 70
    Cantaloupe, 34
    Chocolate Chip Cookie Dough, 57
    Chocolate Spice, 58
    Chocolate Walnut, 8
    Cinnamon Stick, 62
    Classic Chocolate, 8
    Classic Strawberry, 9
    Classic Vanilla, 7

Coconut, 14
Coconut Candy Bar, 26
Dark Chocolate Cheesecake, 92
Deb's Your Choice, 91
Double Chocolate Walnut, 8
Double Coconut, 14
Eggnog, 79
Fig, 69
Fruitcake, 80
Ginger Peach, 25
Ginger Plum, 40
Grasshopper, 84
Green Tea, 90
Hazelnut, 87
Honey Vanilla, 35
Island Delight, 43
Key Lime, 32
Kiss Me Again Chocolate, 73
Maple Cream, 21
Maple Pecan, 21
Maple Walnut, 21
Margarita, 32
Mint Almond, 74
Mint Chocolate Chip, 74
Mint Dark Chocolate, 74
Mocha, 85
Mocha Chip, 85
Nanaimo, 22

Orange Cream with Spiced
    Pecans, 60
Orange Spiced Tea, 55
Peanut Butter, 30
Peanut Butter Chip, 30
Pecan Praline, 56
Peppermint, 77
Persimmon, 61
Pistachio, 12
Port Wine, 76
Pumpkin Cheesecake, 68
Pumpkin Chip, 52
Pumpkin Pie, 52
Pumpkin Spice, 52
Quick Eggnog, 79
Raspberry Cheesecake, 20
Raspberry Mascarpone, 20
Raspberry Truffle, 20
Red Currant, 88
Red Wine, 76
Rocky Road, 31
Rootbeer, 65
Rum Raisin, 83
Spearmint, 77
Spice, 58
Spiced Apple, 51
Spiced Oatmeal Raisin Cookie
    Dough, 58

Spumoni, 10
Strawberry Cheesecake, 11
Strawberry Chocolate Chip, 9
Strawberry Pie, 9
Suzy's Your Choice, 48
Tiramisu, 81
Toasted Almond, 64
Triple Chocolate Overload, 89
Vanilla Bean, 86
Walnut Spice, 58
White Chocolate Almond, 82
White Chocolate Cherry, 78
White Chocolate Macadamia Nut, 82
White Chocolate Nut Ice Cream, 78

Ices

Blueberry, 19
Cider, 54
Citrus, 36
Cranberry, 53
Honey Grapefruit, 36
Mimosa, 75
Painkiller, 17
Peachy Wine, 18
Plum Wine, 18
Strawberry Daiquiri, 16
Island Delight Ice Cream, 43

Key Lime Ice Cream, 32

Kiss Me Again Chocolate Ice Cream, 73
Kiwi Delight Sherbet, 37

Lemon Sherbet, 15
Lime Sherbet, 13

Mango Gelato, 45
Maple Cream Ice Cream, 21
Maple Pecan Ice Cream, 21
Maple Walnut Ice Cream, 21
Margarita Ice Cream, 32
Mimosa Ice, 75
Mint Almond Ice Cream, 74
Mint Chocolate Chip Ice Cream, 74
Mint Dark Chocolate Ice Cream, 74
Mixed Berry Sorbet, 38
Mocha Cappucino Gelato, 66
Mocha Chip Ice Cream, 85
Mocha Ice Cream, 85

Nanaimo Ice Cream, 22

Orange Cream Ice Cream with Spiced
    Pecans, 60
Orange Sherbet, 33
Orange Spiced Tea Ice Cream, 55

Painkiller Ice, 17

Papaya Gelato, 45
Peach Sherbet, 42
Peachy Wine Ice, 18
Peanut Butter Chip Ice Cream, 30
Peanut Butter Ice Cream, 30
Pecan Praline Ice Cream, 56
Peppermint Ice Cream, 77
Persimmon Ice Cream, 61
Pineapple Sherbet, 23
Pistachio Ice Cream, 12
Plum Wine Ice, 18
Port Wine Ice Cream, 76
Pumpkin Cheesecake Ice Cream, 68
Pumpkin Chip Ice Cream, 52
Pumpkin Pie Ice Cream, 52
Pumpkin Spice Ice Cream, 52

Raspberry Cheesecake Ice Cream, 20
Raspberry Mascarpone Ice Cream, 20
Raspberry Sorbet, 38
Raspberry Truffle Ice Cream, 20
Red Currant Ice Cream, 88
Red Wine Ice Cream, 76
Rocky Road Ice Cream, 31
Rootbeer Ice Cream, 65
Rootbeer Sherbet, 44
Rum Raisin Ice Cream, 83

Sherbets
    Cherry, 24
    Chocolate Cherry, 24
    Cream Soda, 44
    Kiwi Delight, 37
    Lemon, 15
    Lime, 13
    Orange, 33
    Peach, 42
    Pineapple, 23
    Rootbeer, 44
Sorbets
    Apple Cinnamon, 59
    Blackberry, 38
    Cranberry, 67
    Cranberry Raspberry, 67
    Gingered Pear, 59
    Mixed Berry, 38
    Raspberry, 38
    Strawberry, 38
    Watermelon, 41
Spearmint Ice Cream, 77
Spice Ice Cream, 58
Spiced Apple Ice Cream, 51
Spiced Oatmeal Raisin Cookie Dough Ice
    Cream, 58
Spumoni Ice Cream, 10

Strawberry Cheesecake Ice Cream, 11
Strawberry Chocolate Chip Ice Cream, 9
Strawberry Daiquiri Ice, 16
Strawberry Pie Ice Cream, 9
Strawberry Sorbet, 38
Sunset Gelato, 46
Suzy's Your Choice Ice Cream, 48

Tiramisu Ice Cream, 81
Toasted Almond Ice Cream, 64
Triple Chocolate Overload Ice Cream, 89

Vanilla Bean Ice Cream, 86

Walnut Spice Ice Cream, 58
Watermelon Sorbet, 41
White Chocolate Almond Ice Cream, 82
White Chocolate Cherry Ice Cream, 78
White Chocolate Macadamia Nut Ice
    Cream, 82
White Chocolate Nut Ice Cream, 78

Please send additional copies of *Ice Cream for All Seasons* at the cost of $12.95 for each book. *For shipping and handling charges, enclose $3.00 for the first book and $1.00 for each additional book shipped to the same address.* For a limited time, we are autographing all books ordered using this form. If you would like your copies personally autographed, complete the "Autographed Message" section below. If necessary, attach another sheet of paper for additional autographed messages. *Ice Cream for All Seasons makes an excellent gift when accompanied by a new electric ice cream maker!*

_____ copies x 12.95 = Book Total: _____

(Wisconsin residents only) Sales Tax @ 5%: _____

Shipping/Handling Total: _____

Total Amount Enclosed: _____

Ship To: _____

Address: _____

City: _____

State: _____ Zip Code: _____

Autographed Message: _____

_____

_____

Make Check or Money Order payable to:
*ReTreat Publishing*

Send payment and order form to:
*ReTreat Publishing*
*2115 Harvest Drive*
*Appleton, Wisconsin 54914*

(This form may be photocopied)

# Ice Cream for All Seasons

*Photography and cover design by Deb Tomasi*

*Back cover photography by Charles Wise*

*Text design by Jeff Eiden*

*Printed and bound under the direction of Scott Markofski*

*Appleton, Wisconsin*

*ReTreat Publishing*